FOR ORGANS, PIANOS & ELECTRONIC KEYBOARDS

214

MW00782612

ISBN 0-7935-0160-1

A Joint Publication Of

AND

Exclusively Distributed By

HAL•LEONARD
CORPORATION
7777 W. Bluemound Rd. P.O. Box 13819 Milwaukee, WI 53213

A Caroling We Go

Registration 4
Rhythm: Waltz

Music and Lyrics by
Johnny Marks

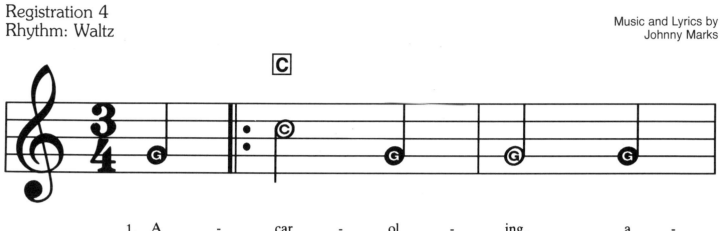

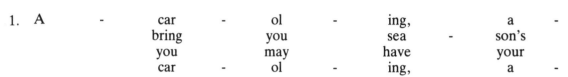

1. A - car - ol - ing, a -
   bring you sea - son's
   you may have your
   car - ol - ing, a -

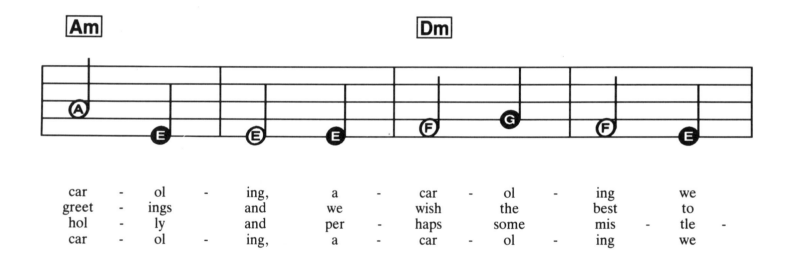

car - ol - ing, a - car - ol - ing we
greet - ings and we wish the best to
hol - ly and per - haps some mis - tle -
car - ol - ing, a - car - ol - ing we

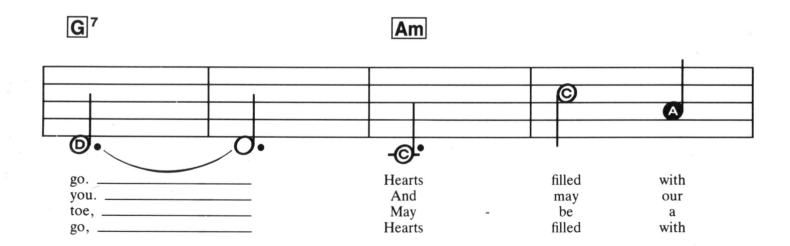

go. _____ Hearts filled with
you. _____ And may our
toe, _____ May - be a
go, _____ Hearts filled with

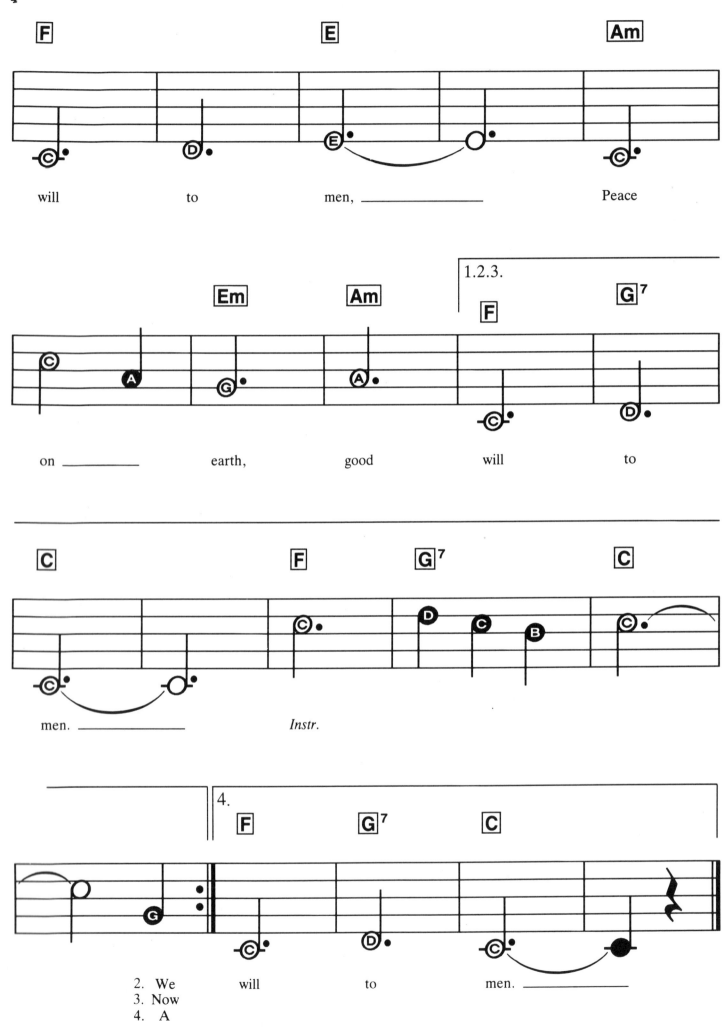

Carol Of The Bells

Registration 2
Rhythm: Waltz

Traditional

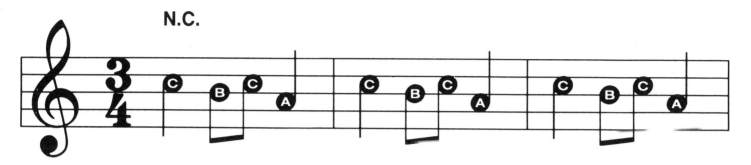

Hark to the bells, Hark to the bells, Tell - ing us all

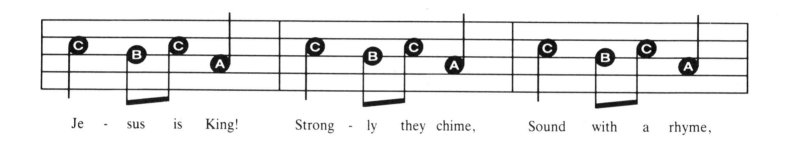

Je - sus is King! Strong - ly they chime, Sound with a rhyme,

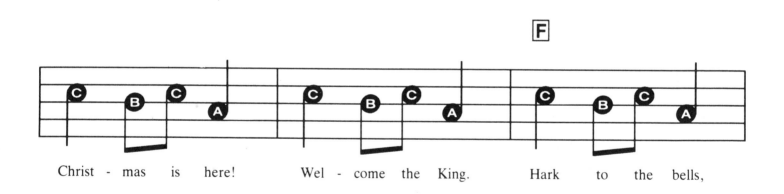

Christ - mas is here! Wel - come the King. Hark to the bells,

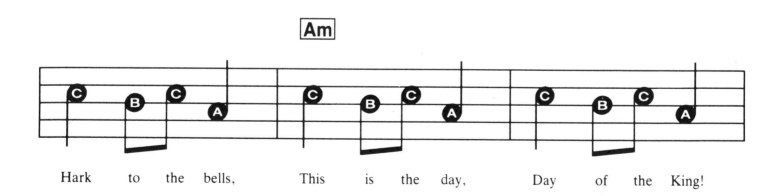

Hark to the bells, This is the day, Day of the King!

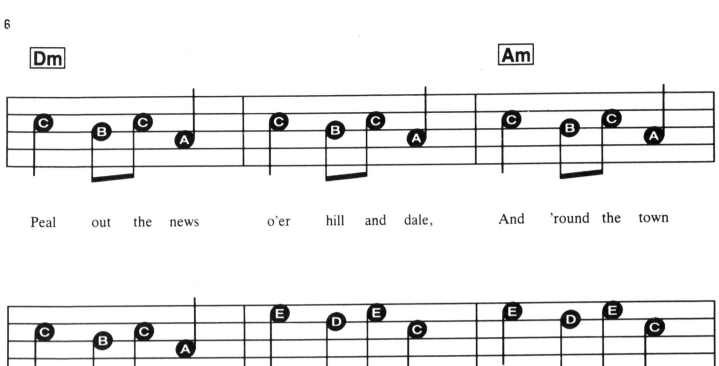

Peal out the news o'er hill and dale, And 'round the town

tell - ing the tale. Hark! to the bells, Hark! to the bells,

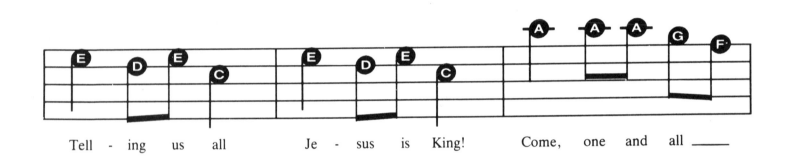

Tell - ing us all Je - sus is King! Come, one and all ___

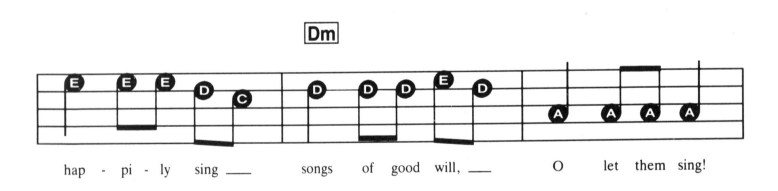

hap - pi - ly sing ___ songs of good will, ___ O let them sing!

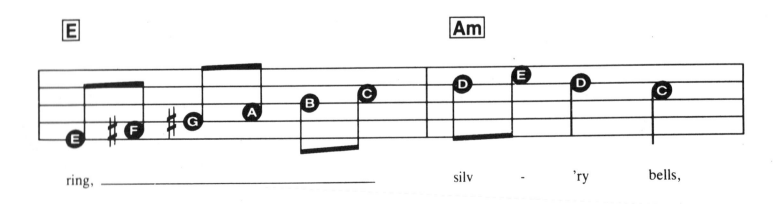

ring, _____ silv - 'ry bells,

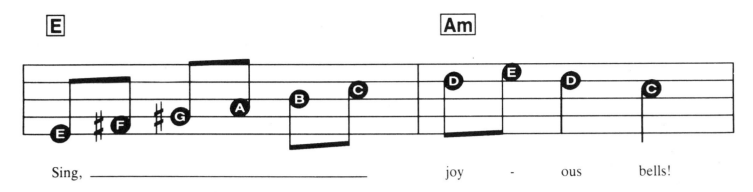

Sing, _____ joy - ous bells!

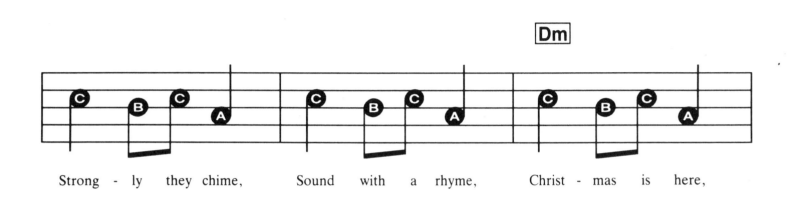

Strong - ly they chime, Sound with a rhyme, Christ - mas is here,

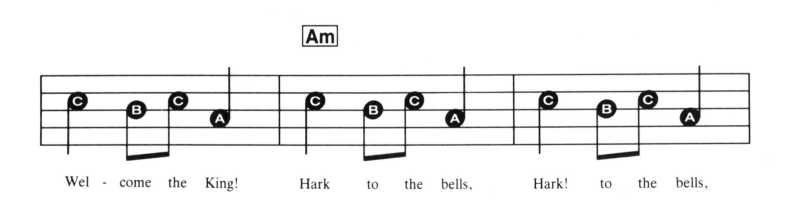

Wel - come the King! Hark to the bells, Hark! to the bells,

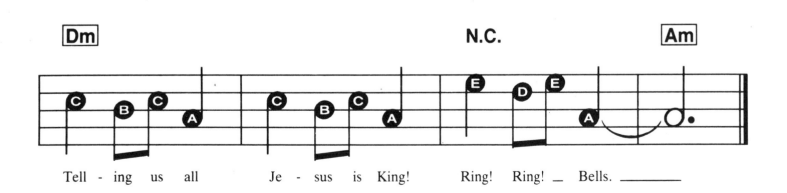

Tell - ing us all Je - sus is King! Ring! Ring! _ Bells. _____

A Marshmallow World

Registration 1
Rhythm: Fox Trot or Swing

Words by Carl Sigman
Music by Peter De Rose

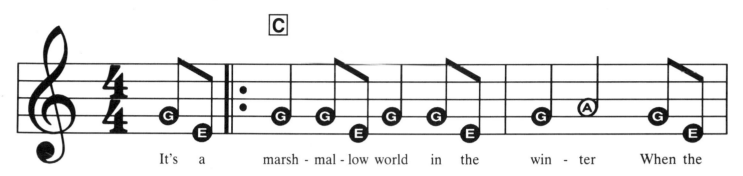

It's a marsh - mal - low world in the win - ter When the

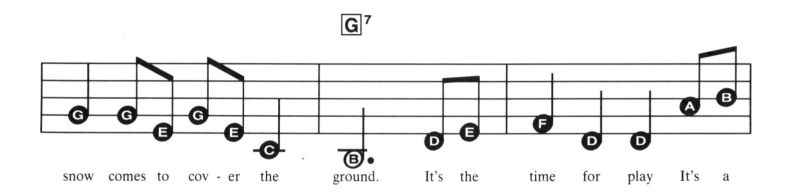

snow comes to cov - er the ground. It's the time for play It's a

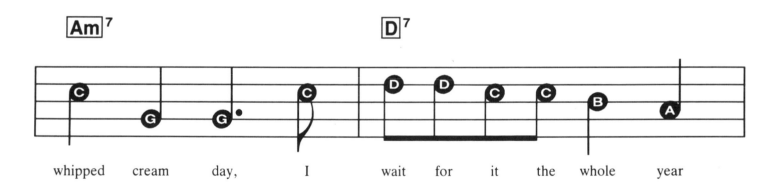

whipped cream day, I wait for it the whole year

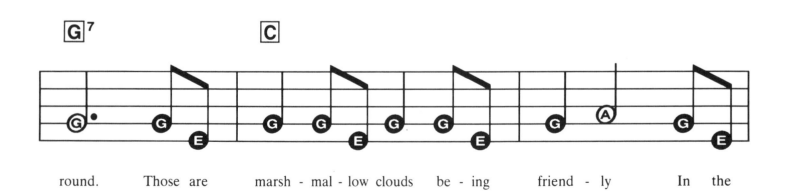

round. Those are marsh - mal - low clouds be - ing friend - ly In the

9

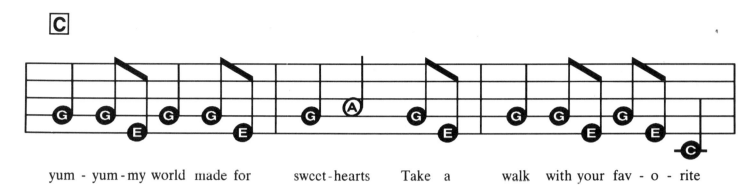

yum - yum - my world made for sweet-hearts   Take a   walk   with your fav - o - rite

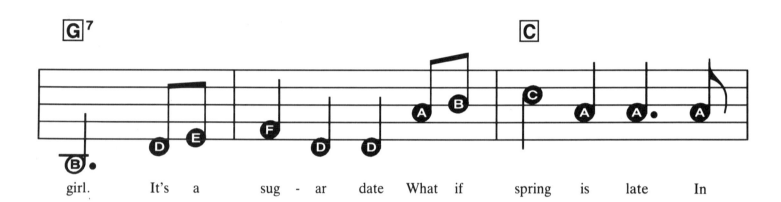

girl.   It's   a   sug - ar   date   What if   spring   is   late   In

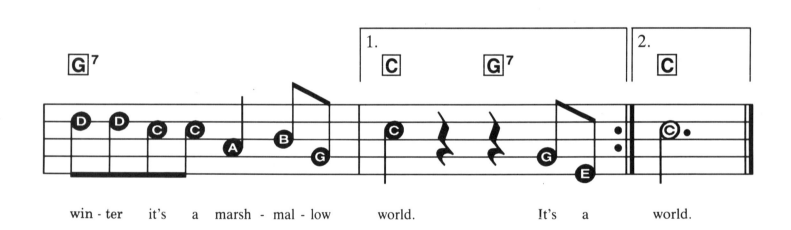

win - ter   it's   a   marsh - mal - low   world.   It's   a   world.

Here Comes Santa Claus
(Right Down Santa Claus Lane)

Registration 2
Rhythm: Fox Trot or Swing

Words and Music by Gene Autry
and Oakley Haldeman

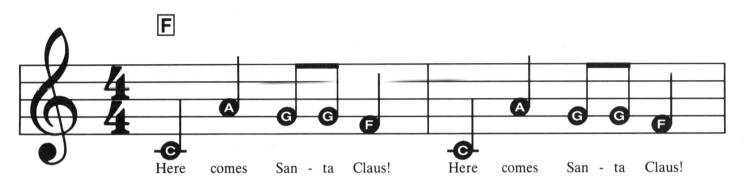

Here comes San - ta Claus! Here comes San - ta Claus!

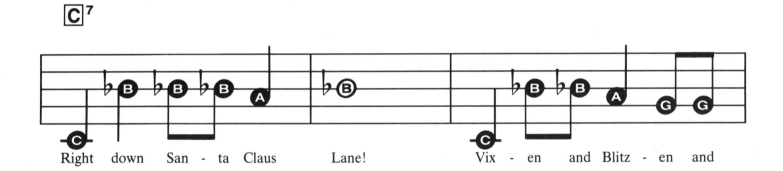

Right down San - ta Claus Lane! Vix - en and Blitz - en and

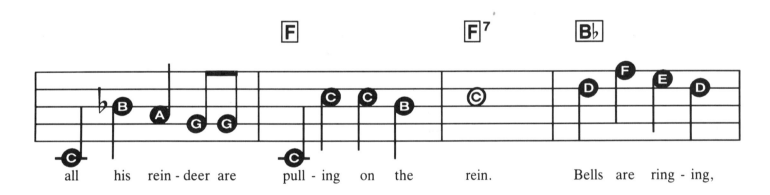

all his rein - deer are pull - ing on the rein. Bells are ring - ing,

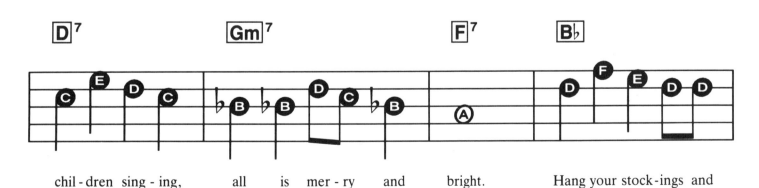

chil - dren sing - ing, all is mer - ry and bright. Hang your stock - ings and

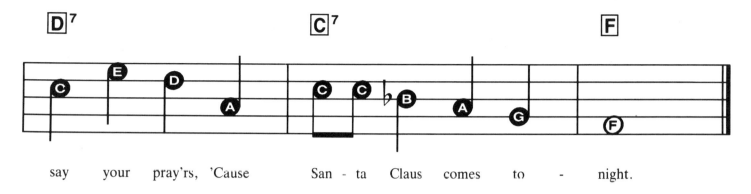

say your pray'rs, 'Cause San - ta Claus comes to - night.

Have Yourself A Merry Little Christmas

Registration 7
Rhythm: Fox Trot or Swing

Words and Music by Ralph Blane
and Hugh Martin

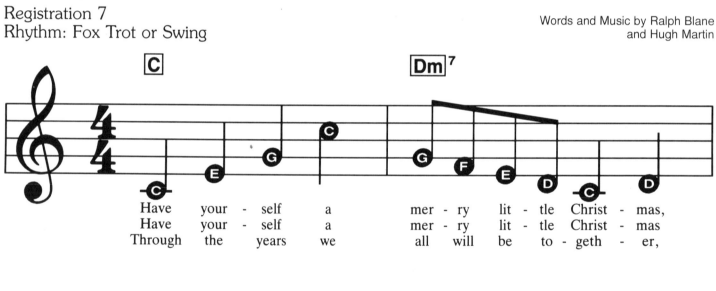

Have your - self a mer - ry lit - tle Christ - mas,
Have your - self a mer - ry lit - tle Christ - mas
Through the years we all will be to - geth - er,

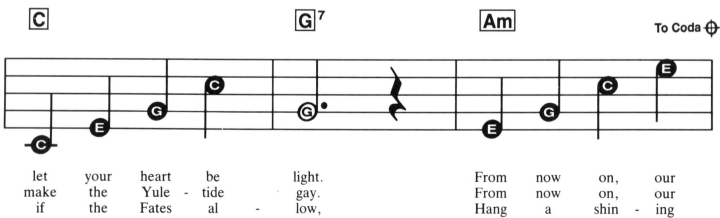

let your heart be light. From now on, our
make the Yule - tide gay. From now on, our
if the Fates al - low, Hang a shin - ing

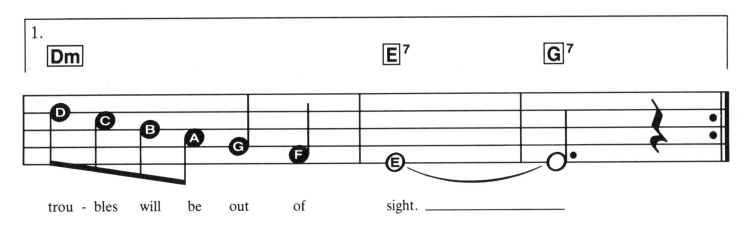

trou - bles will be out of sight. _____

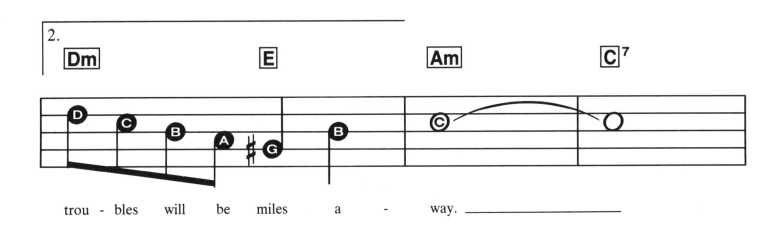

trou - bles will be miles a - way. _____

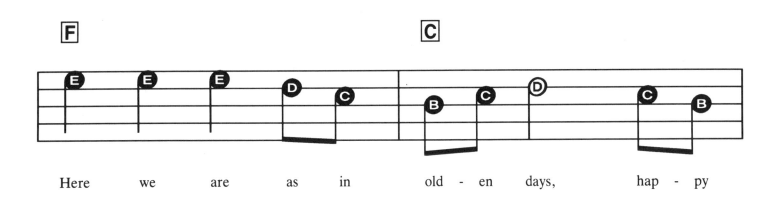

Here we are as in old - en days, hap - py

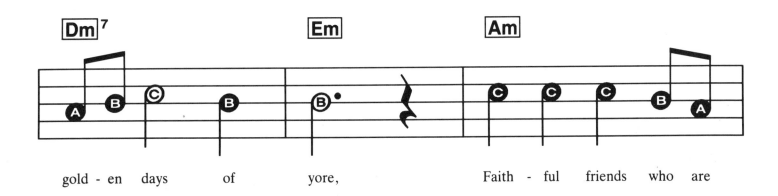

gold - en days of yore, Faith - ful friends who are

14

D.C. al Coda
(Return to beginning
Play to ⊕ and
Skip to Coda)

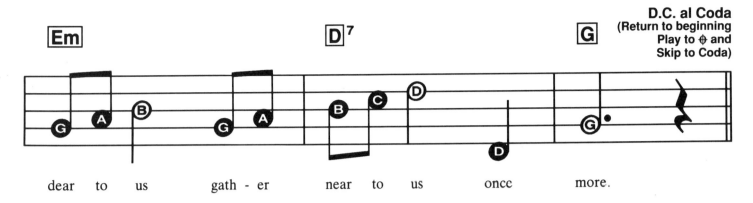

dear   to   us   gath - er   near   to us   once   more.

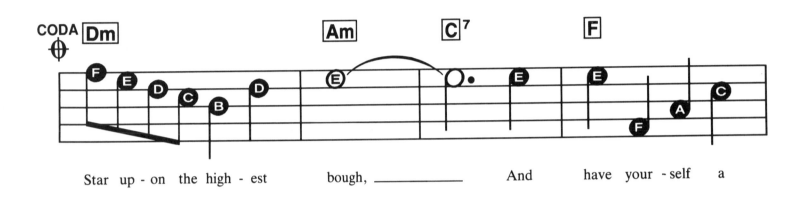

Star up - on the high - est   bough, _____   And   have your - self   a

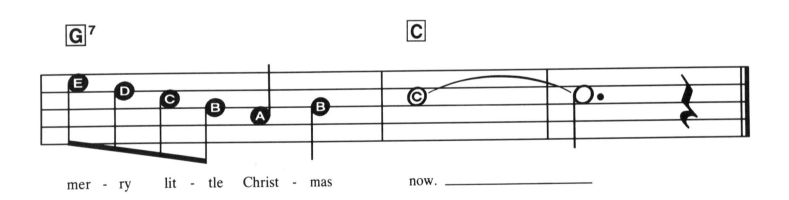

mer - ry   lit - tle Christ - mas   now. _____

A Merry, Merry Christmas To You

Registration 1
Rhythm: Waltz

Music and Lyrics by
Johnny Marks

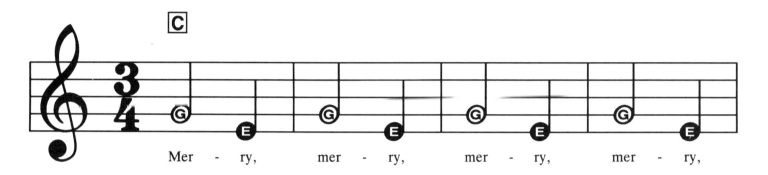

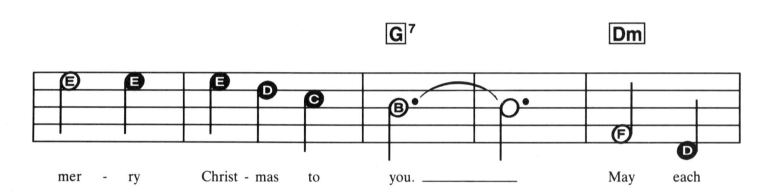

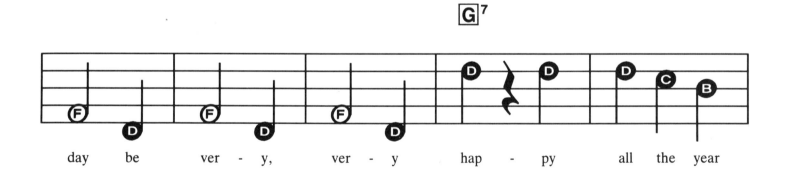

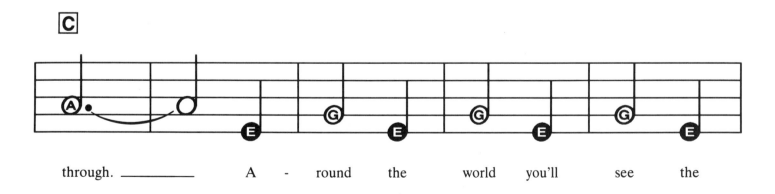

D.C. al Coda
(Return to beginning
Play to ⊕ and
Skip to Coda)

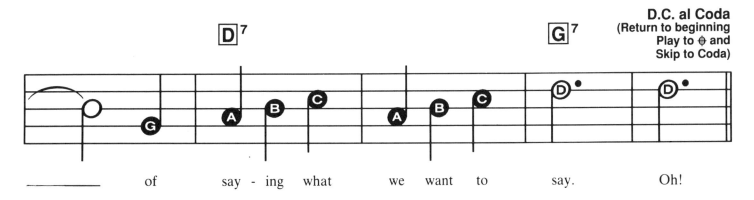

_____ of say - ing what we want to say. Oh!

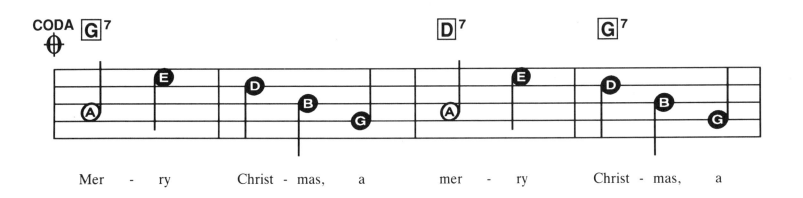

CODA

Mer - ry Christ - mas, a mer - ry Christ - mas, a

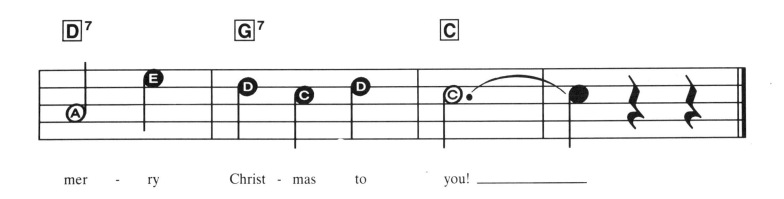

mer - ry Christ - mas to you! _____

The Most Wonderful Day Of The Year

Registration 2
Rhythm: Waltz

Music and Lyrics by
Johnny Marks

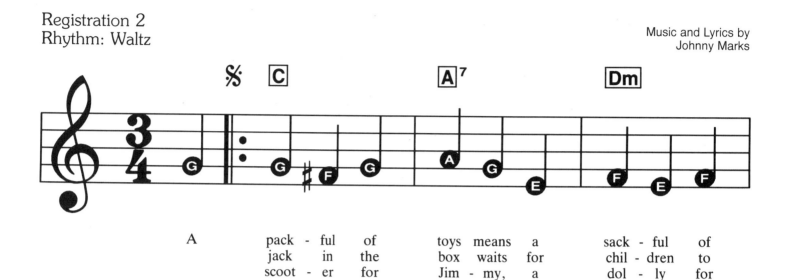

A   pack - ful   of   toys   means   a   sack - ful   of
jack   in   the   box   waits   for   chil - dren   to
scoot - er   for   Jim - my,   a   dol - ly   for

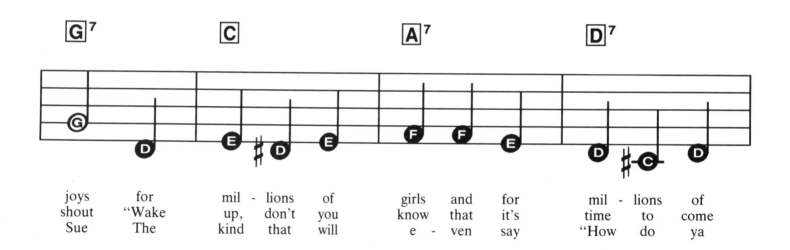

joys   for   mil - lions   of   girls   and   for   mil - lions   of
shout   "Wake   up,   don't   you   know   that   it's   time   to   come
Sue   The   kind   that   you   will   e - ven   say   "How   do   ya

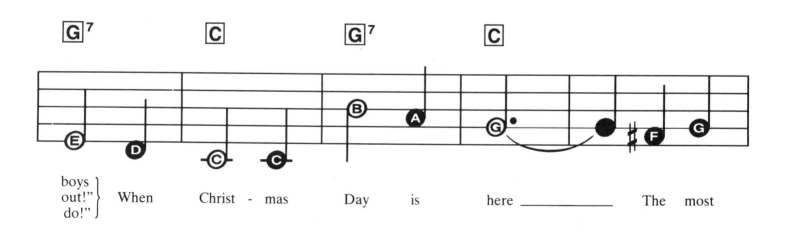

boys
out!"}   When   Christ - mas   Day   is   here _____   The   most
do!"}

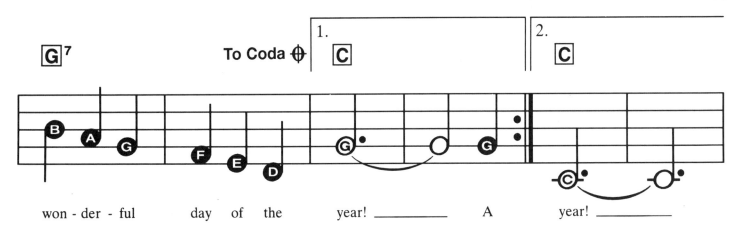

won - der - ful   day   of   the   year! _____ A   year! _____

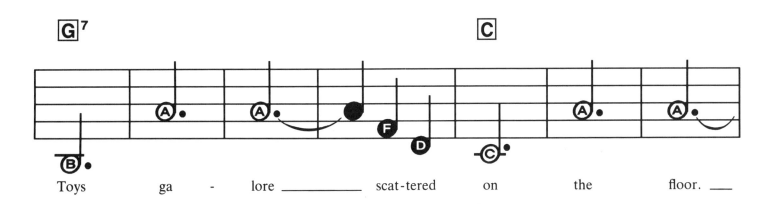

Toys   ga -   lore _____ scat-tered   on   the   floor. __

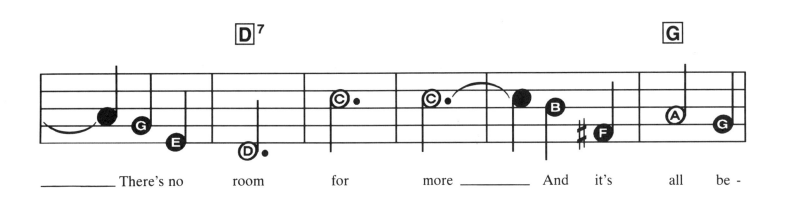

_____ There's no   room   for   more _____ And   it's   all   be -

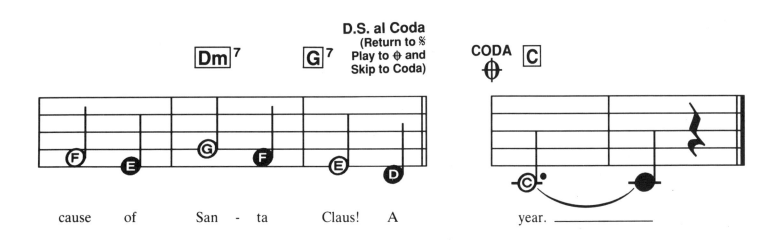

cause   of   San -   ta   Claus! A   year. _____

Silver Bells
from the Paramount Picture THE LEMON DROP KID

Registration 8
Rhythm: Waltz

Words and Music by Jay Livingston
and Ray Evans

hear: _____
hear: _____ }
Sil - ver bells, _____ sil - ver bells, _

_____ It's Christ - mas time in the cit - y. _

_____ Ring - a - ling, _____ hear them ring, _____

1.
soon it will be Christ - mas day. _____ Strings of

2.
day. *(Instrumental)*

Baby Brother

Registration 9
Rhythm: Fox Trot or Swing

Words and Music by Vaughn Horton
and Willie Evans

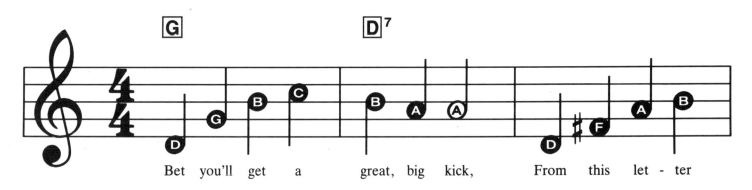

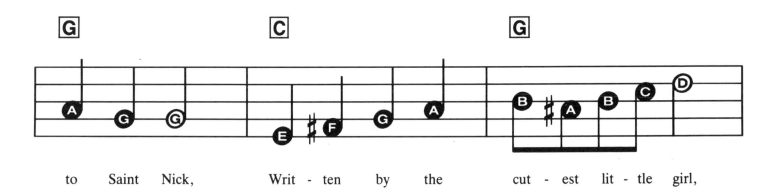

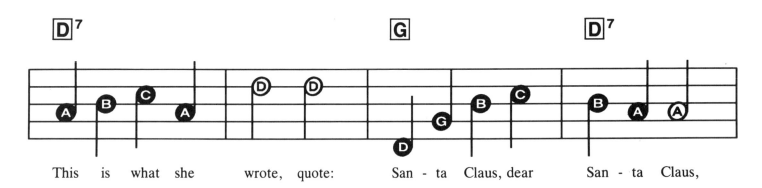

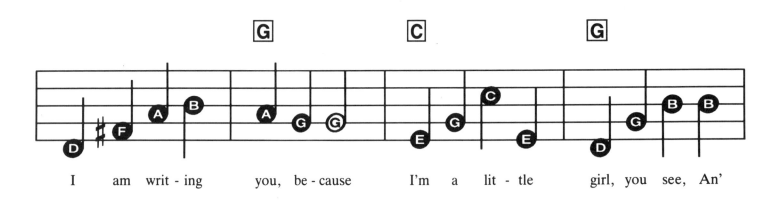

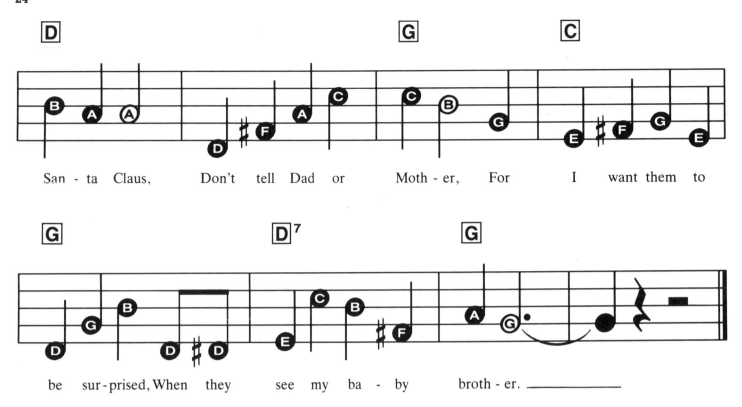

San - ta Claus, Don't tell Dad or Moth - er, For I want them to

be sur - prised, When they see my ba - by broth - er. _____

Do You Hear What I Hear

Registration 1
Rhythm: March

Words and Music by Noel Regney
and Gloria Shayne

1. Said the night ___ wind to the lit - tle lamb,
lit - tle lamb to the shep - herd boy,
shep - herd boy to the might - y king,

Do you see what I see? _____ 'Way up in the sky, lit - tle
Do you hear what I hear? _____ Ring - ing thru the sky, shep - herd
Do you hear what I hear? _____ In your pal - ace warm, might - y

lamb,	Do	you	see	what	I	see?	A	star,	a	star,
boy,	Do	you	hear	what	I	hear?	A	song,	a	song,
king,	Do	you	know	what	I	know?	A	child,	a	child,

danc - ing	in	the	night,	With	a	tail	as	big	as	a
high	a - bove	the	tree,	With	a	voice	as	big	as	the
shiv - ers	in	the	cold?;	Let	us	bring	him	sil - ver	and

1.2.

kite,	With	a	tail	as	big	as	a	kite.	2. Said the
sea,	With	a	voice	as	big	as	the	sea.	3. Said the
gold,	Let	us	bring	him	sil - ver	and	gold.	

3.

| Said | the | king | to | the | peo - ple | ev - 'ry - where, |

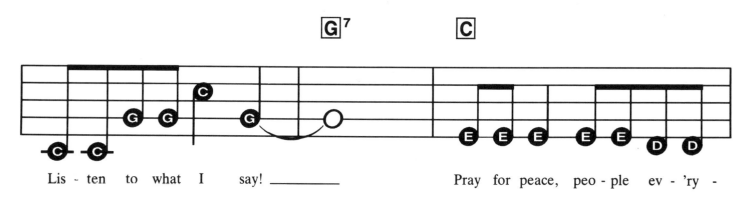

Lis - ten to what I say! _____ Pray for peace, peo - ple ev - 'ry -

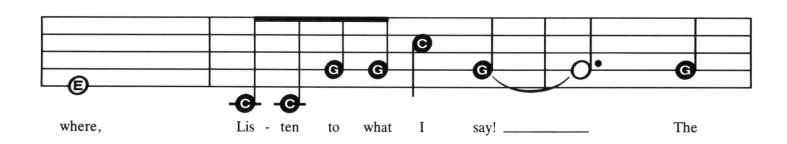

where, Lis - ten to what I say! _____ The

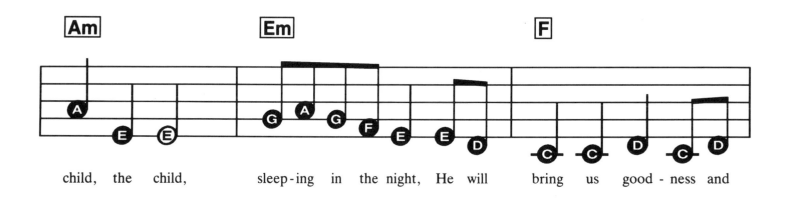

child, the child, sleep-ing in the night, He will bring us good - ness and

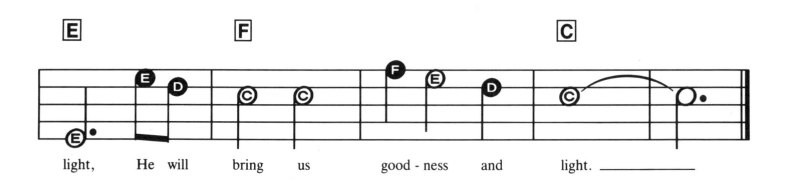

light, He will bring us good - ness and light. _____

Sleigh Ride

Registration 2
Rhythm: Fox Trot or Swing

Words by Mitchell Parrish
Music by Leroy Anderson

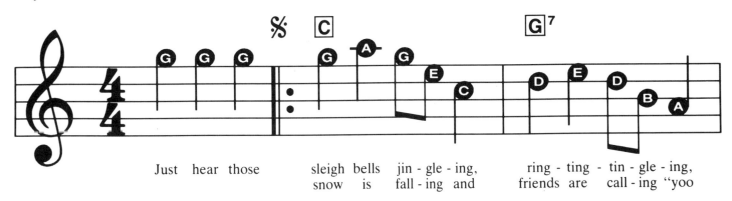

Just hear those sleigh bells jin - gle - ing, ring - ting - tin - gle - ing,
snow is fall - ing and friends are call - ing "yoo

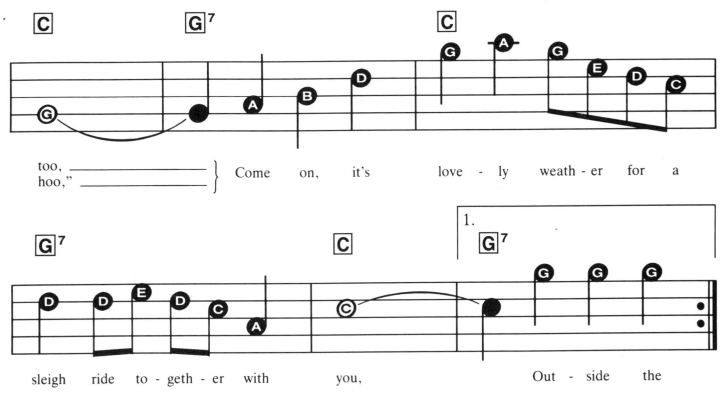

too, _____ } Come on, it's love - ly weath - er for a
hoo," _____ }

sleigh ride to - geth - er with you,

Out - side the

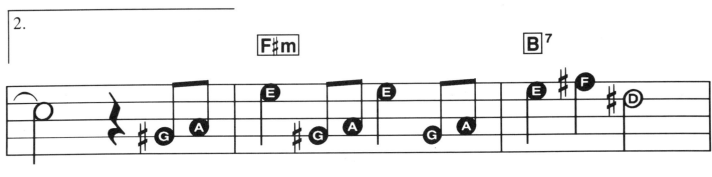

Gid - dy - yap, gid - dy - yap, gid - dy - yap, let's go,

28

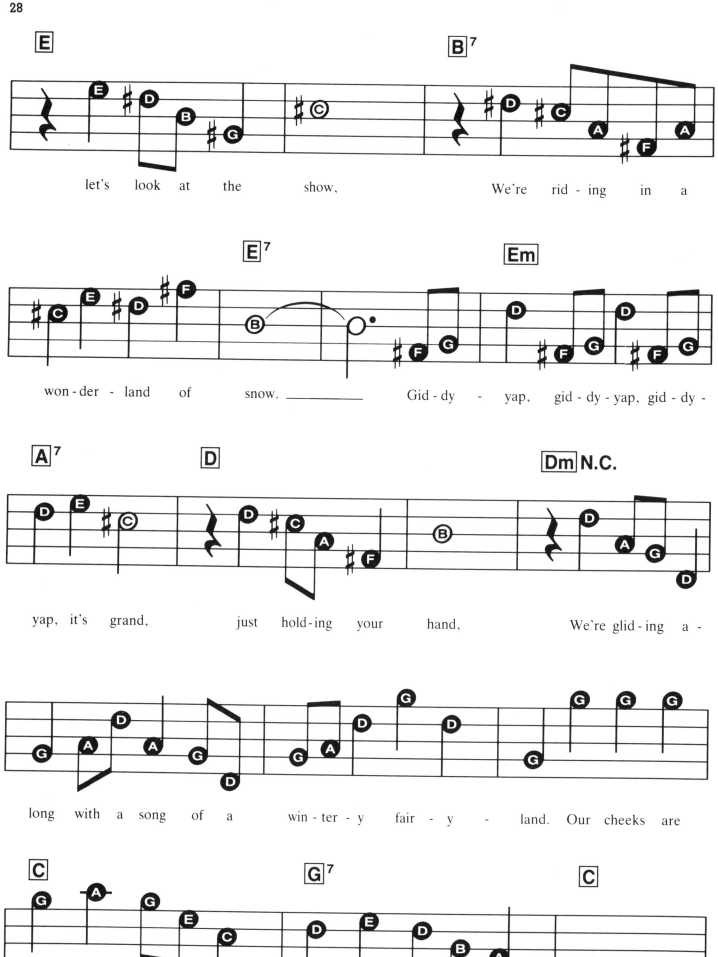

We're snug-gled up to-geth-er like two birds of a feath-er would be. _____ Let's take that road be-fore us and sing a chor-us or two, _____ Come on, it's love-ly weath-er for a sleigh ride to-geth-er with you. _____ There's a

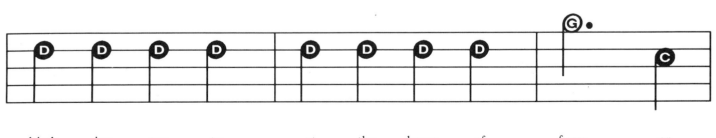

birth-day par-ty at the home of farm-er

30

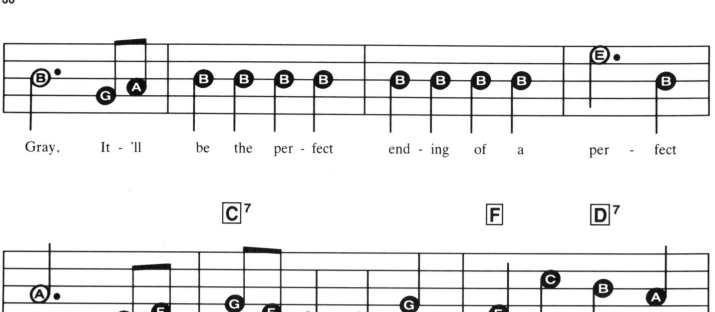

Gray, It - 'll be the per - fect end - ing of a per - fect

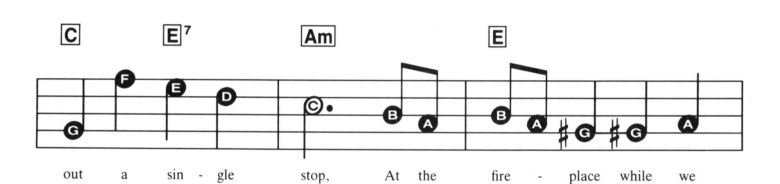

day, We'll be sing - ing the songs we love to sing with -

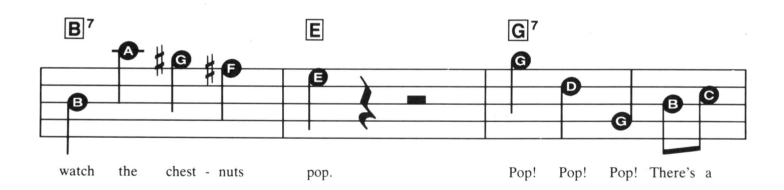

out a sin - gle stop, At the fire - place while we

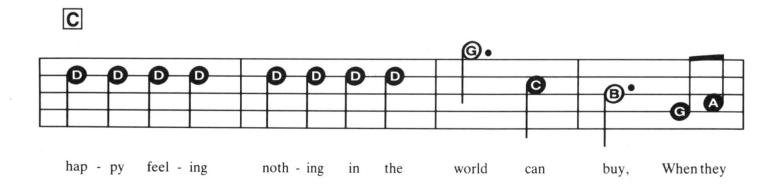

watch the chest - nuts pop. Pop! Pop! Pop! There's a

C

hap - py feel - ing noth - ing in the world can buy, When they

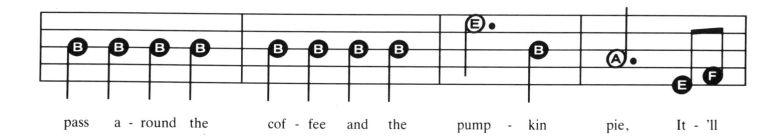

pass a - round the cof - fee and the pump - kin pie, It - 'll

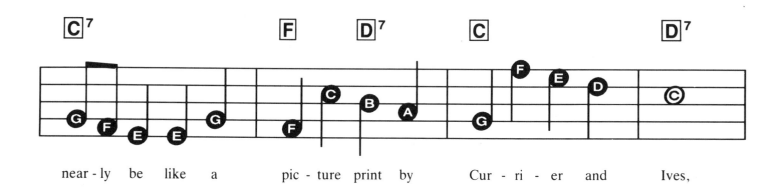

near - ly be like a pic - ture print by Cur - ri - er and Ives,

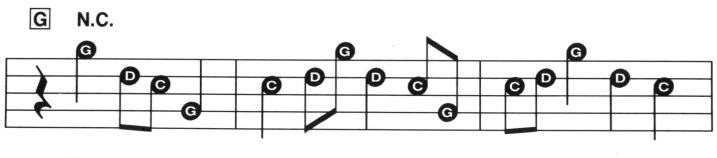
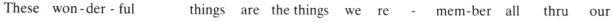

These won - der - ful things are the things we re - mem-ber all thru our

D.S. al Coda
(Return to %
Play to ⊕ and
Skip to Coda)

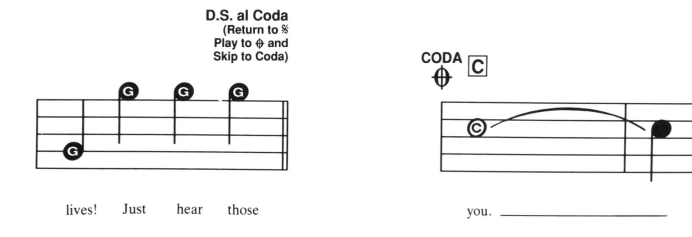

lives! Just hear those

CODA

you. _____

Jingle, Jingle, Jingle

Registration 3
Rhythm: Fox Trot or Swing

Music and Lyrics by
Johnny Marks

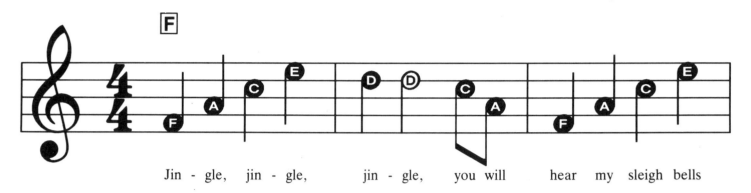

Jin - gle, jin - gle, jin - gle, you will hear my sleigh bells

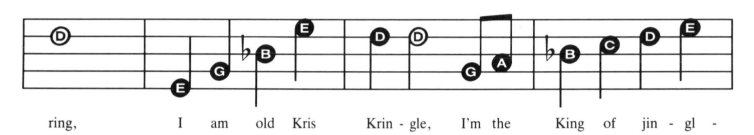

ring, I am old Kris Krin - gle, I'm the King of jin - gl -

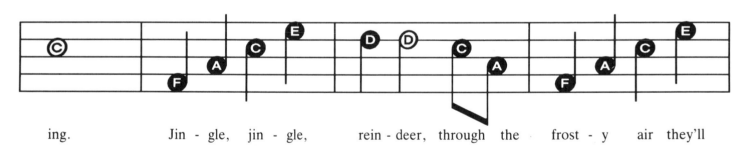

ing. Jin - gle, jin - gle, rein - deer, through the frost - y air they'll

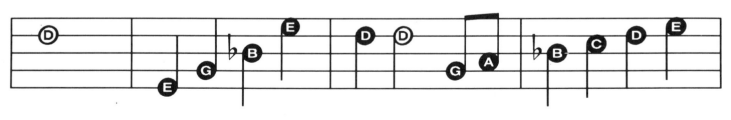

go, They are not just plain deer, they're the fast - est deer I

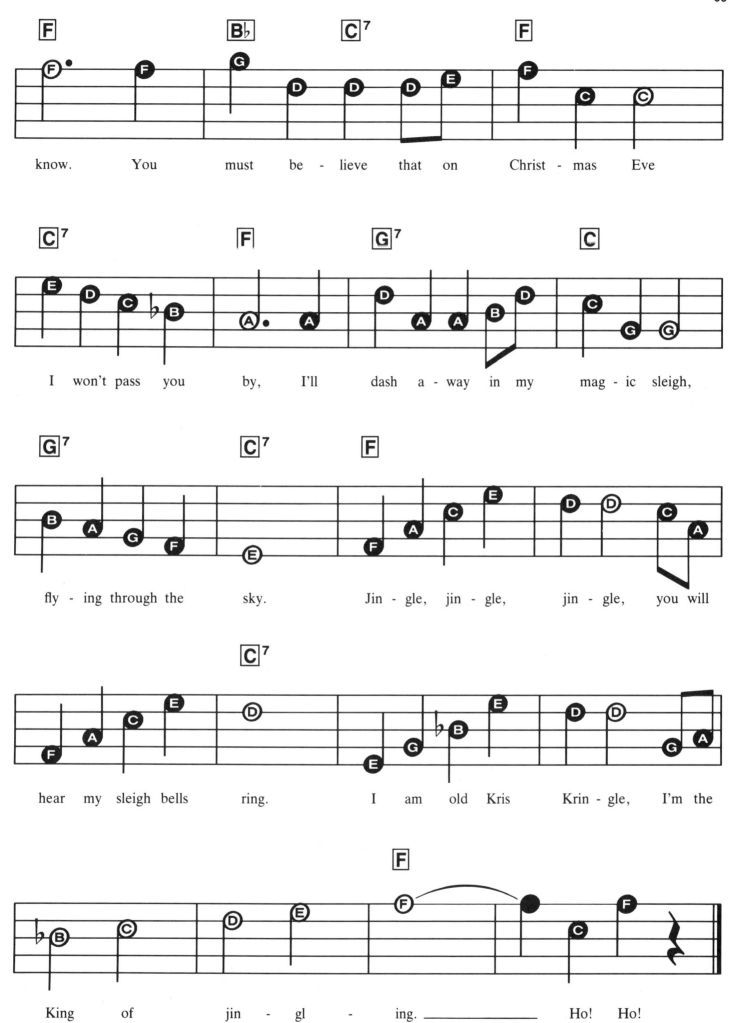

Let It Snow! Let It Snow! Let It Snow!

Registration 7
Rhythm: Fox Trot or Swing

Words by Sammy Cahn
Music by Jule Styne

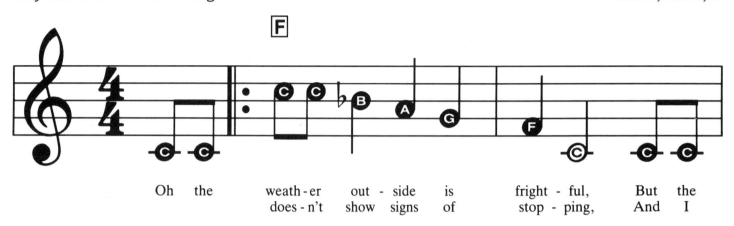

Oh the weath-er out - side is fright - ful, But the
does - n't show signs of stop - ping,   And I

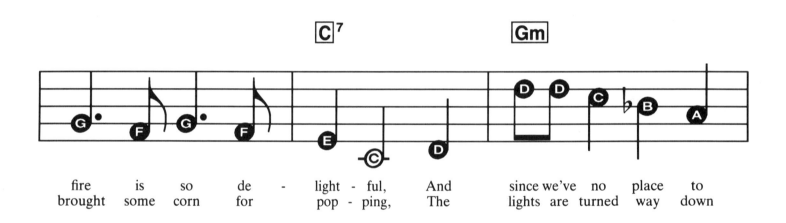

fire is so de - light - ful, And
brought some corn for pop - ping, The

since we've no place to
lights are turned way down

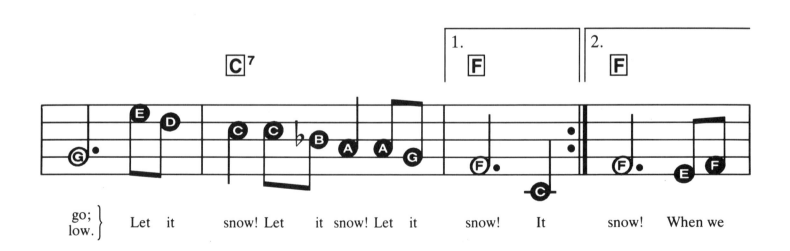

go;
low. } Let it snow! Let it snow! Let it snow! It snow! When we

35

Merry Christmas, Darling

Registration 2
Rhythm: Fox Trot or Swing

Lyric by Frank Pooler
Music by Richard Carpenter

There's Always Tomorrow

Registration 10
Rhythm: Waltz

Music and Lyrics by
Johnny Marks

Rudolph The Red-Nosed Reindeer

Registration 8
Rhythm: Fox Trot or Swing

Music and Lyrics by
Johnny Marks

41

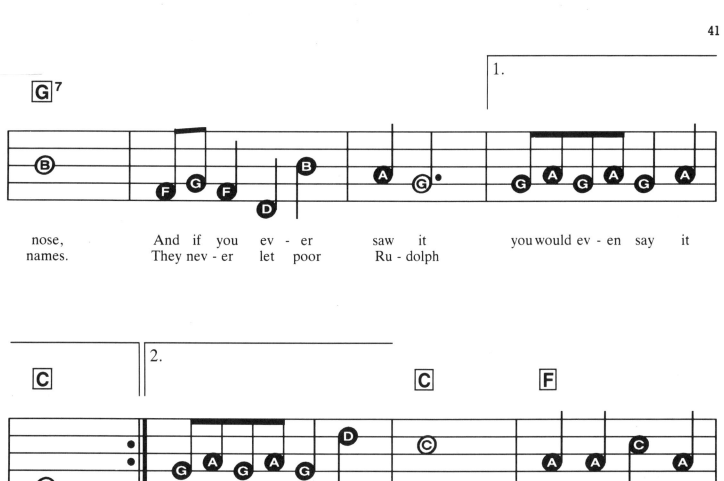

nose,
names.

And if you ev - er saw it
They nev - er let poor Ru - dolph

you would ev - en say it

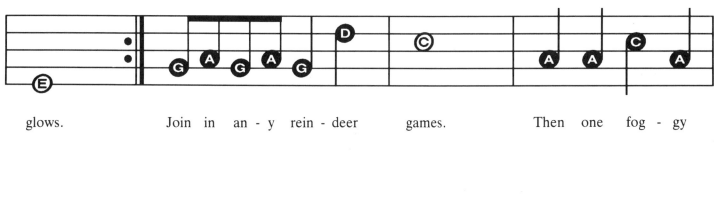

glows.

Join in an - y rein - deer games.

Then one fog - gy

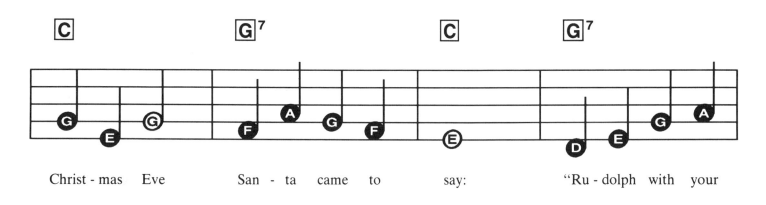

Christ - mas Eve

San - ta came to say:

"Ru - dolph with your

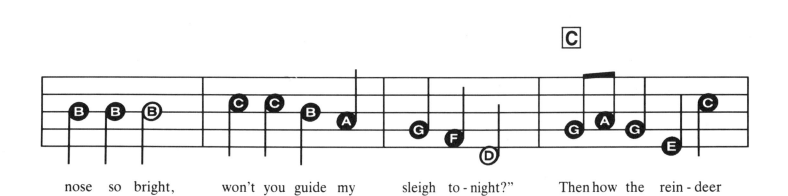

nose so bright,

won't you guide my

sleigh to - night?"

Then how the rein - deer

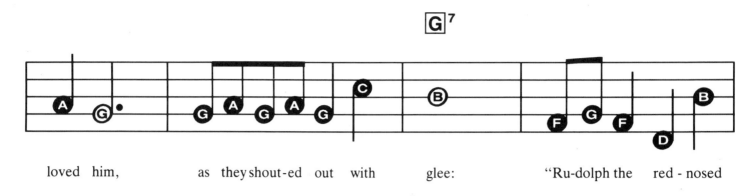

loved him,   as they shout-ed out with   glee: "Ru-dolph the red - nosed

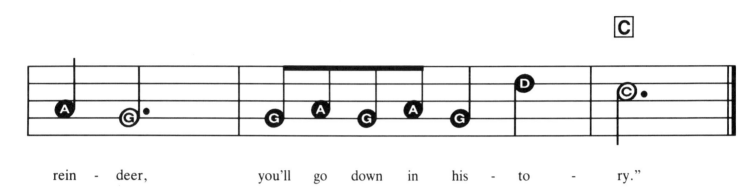

rein - deer,   you'll go down in his - to - ry."

Joyous Christmas

Registration 9
Rhythm: Fox Trot or Swing

Music and Lyrics by
Johnny Marks

Have a   joy - ous Christ - mas,   joy - ous Christ - mas,

fill   your   heart with good   cheer.   Thank the   Lord   a - bove   for
but   don't   fail   to   re -   call   that   a   ti - ny stran - ger
sing   it   loud - ly and   then   pray for   all   your worth   for

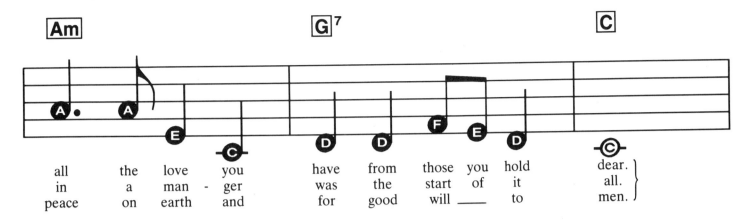

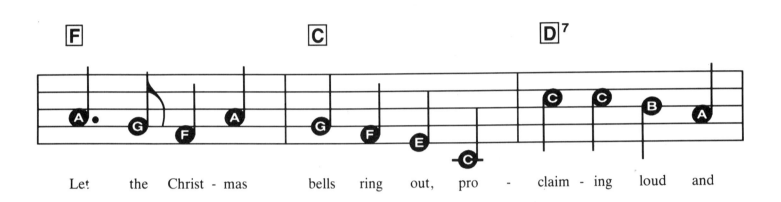

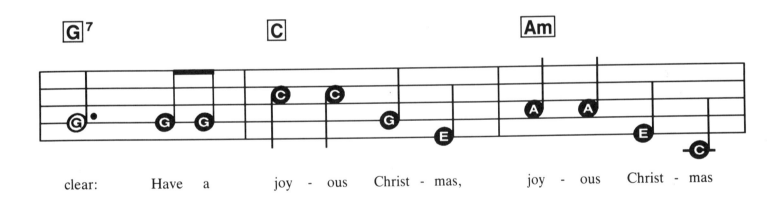

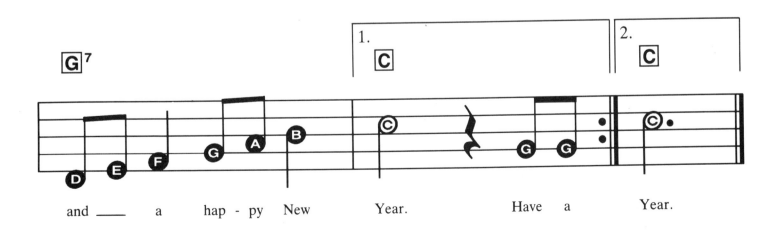

Santa Claus Is Comin' To Town

Registration 7
Rhythm: Fox Trot or Swing

Words by Haven Gillespie
Music by J. Fred Coots

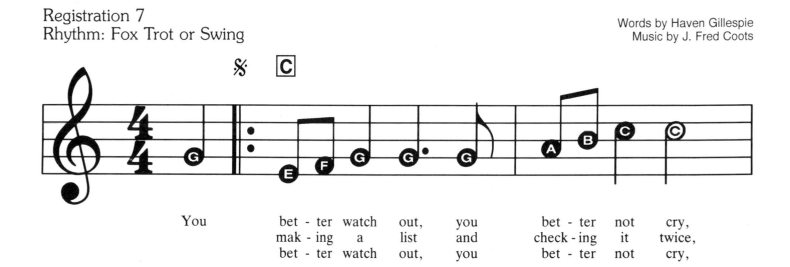

You   bet - ter watch   out,   you   bet - ter   not   cry,
         mak - ing   a   list   and   check - ing it   twice,
         bet - ter watch   out,   you   bet - ter   not   cry,

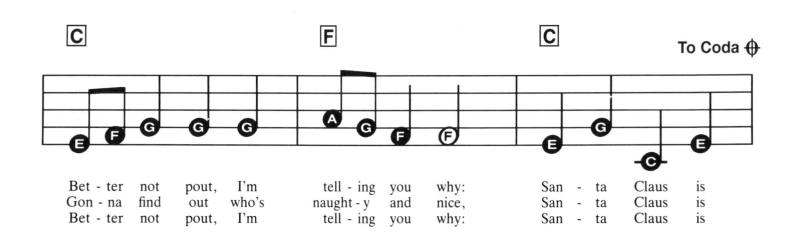

Bet - ter   not   pout,   I'm   tell - ing   you   why: San - ta   Claus   is
Gon - na   find   out   who's   naught - y   and   nice,   San - ta   Claus   is
Bet - ter   not   pout,   I'm   tell - ing   you   why: San - ta   Claus   is

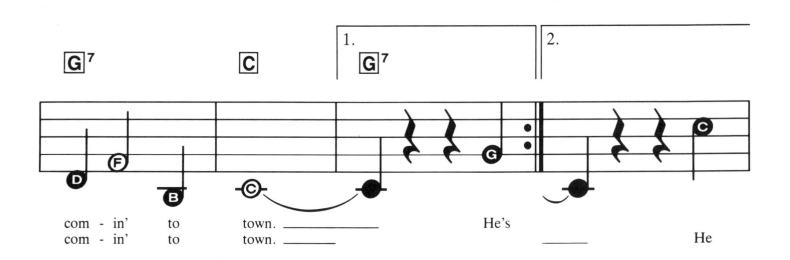

com - in'   to   town. _____   He's
com - in'   to   town. _____   He

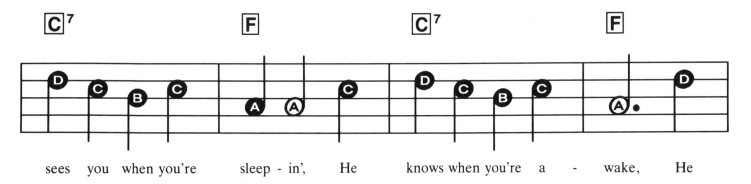

sees you when you're sleep-in', He knows when you're a - wake, He

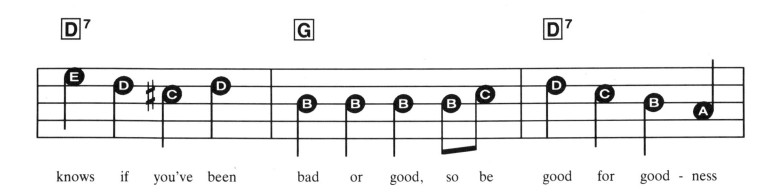

knows if you've been bad or good, so be good for good - ness

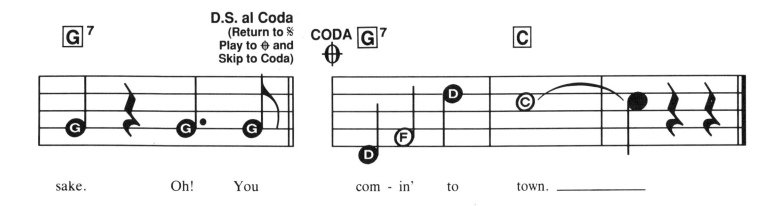

sake. Oh! You com-in' to town. _____

We Are Santa's Elves

Registration 4
Rhythm: Fox Trot or Swing

Music and Lyrics by
Johnny Marks

Ho! Ho! Ho! Ho! Ho! Ho! We are San - ta's elves!

We are San - ta's elves fill - ing San - ta's shelves
We work hard all day, but our work is play.

with a toy for each girl and boy, oh, We are San - ta's elves!
Dolls we try out, see if they cry out,

We've a spec - ial job each year, we don't like to brag,

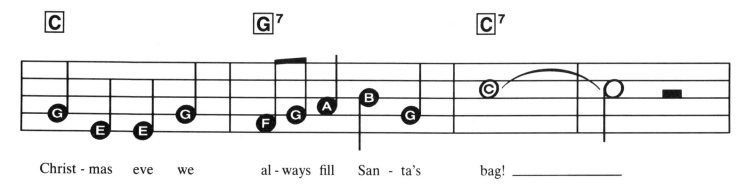

Christ - mas eve we   al - ways fill San - ta's   bag! _____

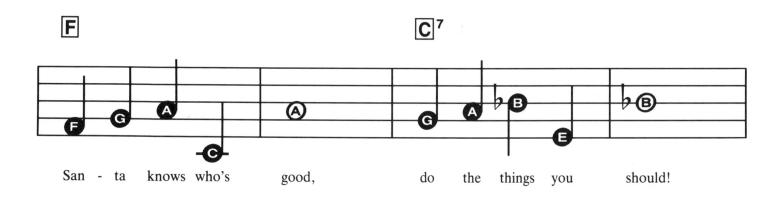

San - ta knows who's   good,   do the things you   should!

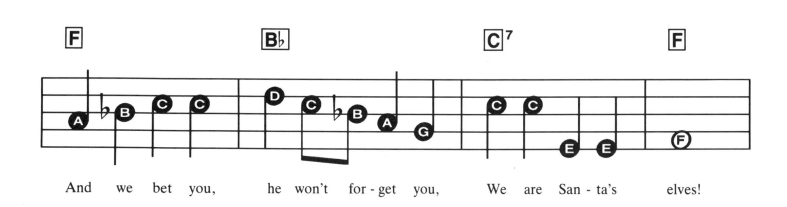

And   we bet you,   he won't for - get you,   We are San - ta's   elves!

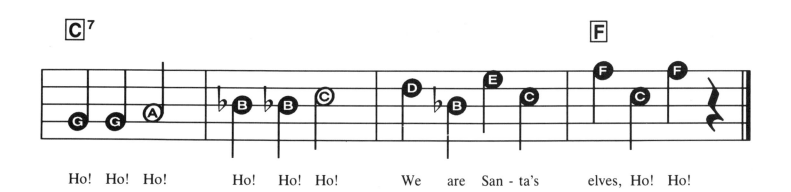

Ho! Ho! Ho!   Ho! Ho! Ho!   We   are San - ta's   elves, Ho! Ho!

Registration Guide

- Match the Registration number on the song to the corresponding numbered category below. Select and activate an instrumental sound available on your instrument.

- Choose an automatic rhythm appropriate to the mood and style of the song. (Consult your Owner's Guide for proper operation of automatic rhythm features.)

- Adjust the tempo and volume controls to comfortable settings.

Registration

1	Flute, Pan Flute, Jazz Flute
2	Clarinet, Organ
3	Violin, Strings
4	Brass, Trumpet, Bass
5	Synth Ensemble, Accordion, Brass
6	Pipe Organ, Harpsichord
7	Jazz Organ, Vibraphone, Vibes, Electric Piano, Jazz Guitar
8	Piano, Electric Piano
9	Trumpet, Trombone, Clarinet, Saxophone, Oboe
10	Violin, Cello, Strings